NOVEMBER, NOVEMBER

NOVEMBER, NOVEMBER

ISABELLA WANG

NIGHTWOOD EDITIONS

2025

1 2 3 4 5 — 29 28 27 26 25

Nightwood Editions
P.O. Box 1779
Gibsons, BC V0N 1V0
Canada
www.nightwoodeditions.com

COVER DESIGN: Angela Yen
TYPOGRAPHY: Rafael Chimicatti

Nightwood Editions acknowledges the support of the Canada Council for the Arts, the Government of Canada, and the Province of British Columbia through the BC Arts Council.

Canada Council for the Arts Conseil des Arts du Canada

This book has been printed on 100% post-consumer recycled paper.

Printed and bound in Canada.

LIBRARY AND ARCHIVES CANADA CATALOGUING IN PUBLICATION
Title: November, November / Isabella Wang.
Names: Wang, Isabella, author
Identifiers: Canadiana (print) 2025021539X | Canadiana (ebook) 20250215403 | ISBN 9780889714847 (softcover) | ISBN 9780889714854 (EPUB)
Subjects: LCGFT: Poetry.
Classification: LCC PS8645.A5317 N68 2025 | DDC C811/.6—dc23

for our loved poets

let us hold them tight
in this realm and the next

CONTENTS

The planet, arium—
atrium, the planet
I have just discovered
in Downtown Toronto.
Stars, stars, stars,
stars. Give me poets,
a hand full of dust
before the skies
fall down.

—Phyllis Webb, "Here I am Reading at the Planetarium" (Unseen and unpublished, transcribed from the audio. Permission attained.)

CONSTELLATIONS

November 2020

Our great land that was dead
Now under the bright sky
Is born again.

—Ai Qing, "Reborn Land"

星座   *constellations*
are ageless suns reborn as stars
in the seats
of a conversation   they can
neither ferry   nor pine
for a different steradian
arrangement   but keep talking

their expositions
depend on the peoples
of lands
and revolutions
seeing them   imagining the *bright sky*
deep futures of their holding
illuminations
until they're gone

mo(u)rnings   how are there
heavens   is there urgency
for us to join the departed still
the skylarks   shepherd
nimbus dunes over sixth snow
and the blue that dawns before
dark's xylem   leaves
its edges with the latewood
and memoir of some pianissimo's firs

is there a thing   as crying
in havens   arrival forgiving
the tin-earthed hearts   their
ghosting of the whistling
stratosphere   for giving them
a night to remember
the tender orbiting of another
year's late growth
and picking up hemlock cones
by the side of the body's
                    capering road

water misses three weeks
filling in six years
of winter leaning's absence

it took time for three movements
and old Chinese proverbs
to gather *connected threads*

among barrels of leaves
stipule and veins laddering
tight mycelial growth   raking

because river constellations
          rove over the sweater
                    of the man wheeling his chair

Li Youran and Ai Qing met
in the beyondery of conifers
like France, Island, a paper clip's
miniature warrens
dividing cylinder folds
out of two pages
and the precipitations of this life

                                        they met
before meeting again
in heaven because of snuck
medicine   friendship
fielding the incarcerated under
revolution's tuberculosis
and corn bread = industrial train dust

some can no longer divide
themselves into halves
to be the poet's split leaf propositions

so we bowl them
with ghost arms into piles
for a while   chestnut leaves

whole with others again

propositions   i could erase
your *and*   with a soft
dinosaur eraser and tell you

in return that the two halves
of what you think are fires
and floods are just feelings—
the weather   expressing
its newfound poems
collaged   re-spored of *light*

that remains unmade   flows out
of the poets who fainted
on stage in New York Buffalo

climate scarves and piano keys
drum against the pharynx
of those with no language to lose

form more intense
friendships love constellating
it makes sense

that through extinction's pulse
there are n-species atmospheric cyan
and rivers all want to live

these slower climbing weeks
of perhaps their last couple months

only the colour blue

will not go extinct
because it was the last pigment
we spent perfecting

and its seeable cellular duplications
of grief have become
Nnedi Okorafor's novella

the last swordfish in water's
nostalgia burns
evolving into a monster

but survives   the rainbow stripes
of gasoline riding
the roof of her home

and catching little fires   like
three fishermen and their dog
planked to the bottom

of the boat   for sixteen hours
as one steered the northwest
axis of the rudder

                              and the others slept unsuspecting

PASSAGE 2

November 2021

for Phyllis and the Loving Crew

white pines   frosted window
won’t let in images of morning

but sunlight until they melt

bus loop   bus drove by me
me stop-signed at another curb

ice crystals write squiggly lines
where previous scratches   on glass

feel everything

                    talked to Phyllis
yesterday   said we both
enjoy the company

of your friendship

          her your anchor
your purpose for escape

                     the city   your work
they are your two ends
          pulling on your Tsawwassen heart
keeping you steady

     youngest of seven siblings
still feel everything

—November 11

— - —

where have the poets gone

the wise   the sager
elders who rocked generations of poets

into their worlds but always insisted
that they do the following

because we are ready
they say   this world they've taught us

that leading is remembering the ones
who ask *are they still thinking about us*

did we at once gather them
and hold them warm this November month

tell them that nights echo thoughts
of how much they are with us

did we gather enough poems
that tell them we still kind of need them

in this world
did we gather a light for them daily

days when we are cold are not ready
to see the places

they've found and are travelling
                                        to be present for

—November 12

— · —

where are the better years

where are the summers and more
comfortable rains forgetting another day

where are the coffee tables and phone call
guests at the enjambments of people's care

stairs we say we miss   some people
the further they are   the longer we long

to reach them
maybe it's a line break   a breath

this lifetime the rains blending
with the mise-en-scène on the ferry ride over

where are the forgotten letters
times she called

and you didn't hear your ringer   now ringing
ringing her way back

they know we need them
the handful who've been leaving us messages

all our lives knowing
we'd only find them   after

the rains travelling with Phyllis   a day later
departing knowing you'd be okay

—November 13

— - —

riling heart

beat slower these

roving winter

mornings

it's okay

to say you feel

a poem

that is different

the winds today

express

the unfinished tempo

of the song

you can't get

yourself to write

just yet

see

you've got

watchful ones

holding

you too

you've got

the trees you

watered

at the roots

swaying

steady and tall

—November 15

— - —

she sensed
past the broken shell   *of her ear*

parts of us needed
to break to feel

less broken   with each other
here are her memories   of you

here are your friendships
                                        forty years later

the bowl collecting
    careful items
                                        stored

storied   it was never *that place of solitude*
for her   the garden of books

sundial   she gave away
but her peopled things

remind you she is here now   still

reminding Phyllis   her people
dialling the sun
                                                    to her near

—November 16

— - —

sun out   this university
is a cold-blooded animal

co-regulates with the thermal
body language
of weather building us indoors

shelters   coffee
lunch office hours   still talking about her

talking found poems of hers
our co-regulation

—November 17

— - —

anarchism left the tired body
re / snow - tired   for the hill frost

wheels of skiddy winter
sun on snow   ices the fragmented

language of auto flows
in any revolution   the sun enters

the room but light sometimes ends
up on the floor   struggles the common

glimmerings of excusable
pause   twenty-five years

thesis on silence while the body
appends an un-failure toward

the unwritable
punctuations of early December

distills the colours of plum   revolution
diamonds from a pattern piece

one purple one red
attach another making designs as I go

loyalty to prince   feminism
exhaust   capitalist continuation

runs out the columns
of cryptography inspiration

tired the feminine
heart-ungoverned body

space resolves to empire citied poetries
the fauna and seaside terraces

medium visions   for the horizon
that body in the living   caesuras to reach

in this life   Canada Council grants
on culture have winters of unexpiry dates

when she left   high energy dreaming
picked up designs to *be* Kropotkin poem

her once-contained caesura
of forms contemplating   "failures"

of the "unfinished"   *horizon*
only in the Russia, Island or France

of this snow motioning earth life

—November 18

— - —

tears salt the good fabric
of her poppy scarf   there is slow quiet

mapped ribbon developments
of our black ice

future winters
everywhere   there is the mildness
of unanticipated clemencies

showing us care
this salt   remnant of her leaving

melting the ground   keeps us safe
while you are driving

for miles   the heart pulses
distances the mind cannot imagine
to cross in a lifetime

why am i crying
grieving a person i've never met

she was in a happy place
far away   Salt Spring Island   you
her most faithful May Day visitor

she is in a happy place
far away   still

what salt crystals thaw the loss
passing of one   not really gone to me

—November 19

— - —

from her   i hope to be the poet
whose lectures   students recall
by her miniature cities of detailed feedback

she inscribed over peak ranges
lines and punctuation
her larger-than-world   wisdoms

they braced
                    books ago

the wiser   older poet
who opens her doors
at the phone line's flutter

though she's made
island the *solitary confinement*
of her unfinished art

let's hope younger generations
will see our work
unfinished   refuse our poetries

        in the margins of their own
world-making   energized coalition

                    there is room

—November 20

— - —

seven-day-mark   then eleven
after eleven   most things we love

are still here with us   it's your birthday
beginning of another seven years

to forge a safe harbour   in her wake
to ember the summer revolutions

of *love and love and love*
poetry isn't

just in the song   of the grieving
but right now it sings

the song of our most   natural grieving
Phyllis knows we've dreamt

of her by the undercommons   of the bridge's
every bodies of water   that without her

we are   canoeing our balance
on the unstable buoyed up maple logs

of a stormy Monday passed   but that
the shell   we brought for her

is collecting water   rimmed and before us
still afloat

there is love

in the dream   Fred   Pauline   Smaro   Diana
sending her emails

in the dream   she'd left us her messages
tomorrow   *hear you*   *and hear Phyllis*

or was it *here*   she wrote
but the shell she kept levitated   for us

teased playfully   to be carried away
with wind of water   if we didn't keep her close

—November 21

— - —

PASSAGE 3

December 2021

UNTITLED

for Otoniya J. Okot Bitek

forgetting's solidarity
is the body remembering

to tie a knot along the polyvagal rivers
of histories some share

witness the body work
of witnessing—a body of work

the collaboration of forms
                collaboration of the senses

beneath parabolic time
is the space of non-linear time

one shares a photograph
and counts down the 100 days

reflection's strength tying
                                is body work

city heartbeat and footnote rhythms
walking water's audible syntax

in the rain when the ground at dew / due
/ dawn recognizes their kin

SOFT

for the poet ferrying to Galiano Island for a reading

there's a bog gathers from the sepia
of earth and bronchial sojourns of a tree over evening of
your travels your first reading

since heat doming pandemic
taking you islands across now accidental ecosystems
of rain rakes last fallen leaves in your

backyard deep futures rising like miniature lily pads
there's the voice of rain announcing fog's body
its silent unperimetered existence your poetry

rafts with the memory of otters and their play
the bevy of others welcoming your poet presence
onto November island heard everything we know

has collected water edging felt-tip sky
longing as bowls after everything else fell asleep
from the palpebrae of a monochrome world ferrying on the backs

of a storm that perspires and falls asleep too
while your walk takes
centuries of earth to form there's the sound

of a bog populating city of raindrops   spelling micro-worlds
under skin's tender margins   the fog taking   you home
has lifted the sky   enough

so your tired   notebook can experience
every droplet of rain as a pencil   inscribing
continuance

through your events   performance and friends
recalling the now's
palpitating
past
rain as
snow's past

palpitating vulnerable   form

TO OTHER CANCER PATIENTS

finding out their diagnosis
near the holidays   it's a beautiful
world   and i'm also
scared to leave it   it's a beautiful
world transformed in night
and five inches of snow   and i'm
halted by it   everywhere
are the feelings i wrote of the
marina / timber mornings of the city
written years ago   never so still
but this time   feeling again
but cannot express   nor hear
nor cry

i walked down
the water written before   muscle
memory asking   what to say
of the fishing boats now
like winter loons
anchoring stoically   their
mast fins to the sky
what to say of anything   now
i know it's not all beautiful

like the new symptoms hurt
and there are people
you love   you won't tell until
the holidays are over   city windows
smashed because the people
without a home are cold   only the ERs
are open   and only you
and one incarcerated patient
got private rooms

this is a white Christmas
you'll never forget   and there's not
an inch of blue in the sky
dawning   yawning quietly
until you open the door   and it's
beautiful again

DESCENDING

for Julia Lunot

i have known you enough
        to understand that when you say

                your life is like a surfboard
trying to ride the waves   you are its only hope
        of staying upright

i don't know everything
                you've been through   i have
        never been surfing

                                but i have tried
to swim the ocean once
                swimming isn't the hard lesson
        we only have to learn once
                in our lives
it's trying to stand back up   when your feet
are being cut by barnacles
                        who've known this world
much longer
                and you have only

        the waves to latch onto
two metres from shore during high tide

                        distance doesn't matter

entropy returns as force viscosity
as ancestors we've left in another land

trying to reach us it makes sense
they try too hard sometimes
we are their descendants

i know you are waiting for another wave
so you can demonstrate a flawless
execution and tell yourself
maybe it will stop hurting after that

but the water
will see the bottom
of your surfboard and think
that your shadows growing taller
along the waves each year
are tidal gifts progressing it too

NOT A SPONGEBOB POEM

for Steve

you are searching to *heal something*
i had forgotten

on the far side
of the receding hill

i saw was
our only refuge

my epistolary caesura
carpools a long horizon of past

future tenses we leave behind
following a basalt grey sedan in New West

soon the water park and mall
in your lit urban Tsawwassen that you say

is a strange mall
because it has Forever 21 and canoes

and guns—i'm thinking it's probably
easier to get licensed for guns

in some cities than a licence for driving
though I should learn that soon

you are both here and not driving
so you don't know that i've failed—

i am pointing out Poplar Island
to my friends and baby Malooky in the car

only after the trees and water
had already left us to join the sunlit rest

of our horizon of past future tenses
and i'm here trying to recreate

a teachable moment that only one of us
has ever successfully taught   meanwhile i

memoried over
how do i be a good teacher like Steve?

Ahmed writes *the history of bodies*
can be rewritten as the history of the reachable

you are not like some horizons
that never let themselves be horizons again

meaning some days we don't get to rewrite
the history of our bodies

some days lessons are not poems
but fingerprints inking at first a map

over years of historical documents
circa Cecily   but to you there's always

a second chance   left of the car
beneath is the bridge   so you can show me the trees

at left's end where
the poplars grow and i'll keep listening—

you say *i don't like commas that much*
and i think that's fine Steve

you've offered me more time to breathe *than* . . .
you are the summer that keeps creating

full bodied—even if those documents
are the solstice for other poets until another spring

— - —

IF, THERE IS TIME

1. Then November came. Then there are no easy beginnings. Life is cut short. Then faced with my own mortality.

2. When news came. When a phone call changes everything. When grief and desire become synonymous with a make-your-own-will kit from Amazon I don't know how to begin to write.

3. One month compiles into thirty letters to loved ones. Thirty love letters all in my head.

4. When I dial numbers on my phone. When I know my news will make some people cry. When someone I know is on their way to the grocery store.

5. I say, Call me back later when you are home, and sitting down. I will wait for your call. Do they already know?

6. People begin lighting candles and pray for me. I disown the future because not caring is easier on the heart than grieving the things I still must do.

7. My essays are incomplete. My professors defer my grade. Then writing's process becomes unfamiliar.

8. My body is unfamiliar. I have no energy, no body mass, no sleep, or the ability to make language with my body. I am homeless too. Better not to give the tumour a permanent place to call home.

9. I stay with several friends. Tsawwassen, Coquitlam, Fairview.

10. The story I have to tell has already been told many times: to me, by me, by others who've made the same phone calls that have made their loved ones cry. This story I am silently sneaking into the basement of the hospital library between a book.

11. I am here for an internal specialist consult, left here to wait.

12. Some stories have no rising actions, no plot, no rest in the silences, no relief in the resolution of some long-anticipated denouement. I want there to be a record of this kind of story here on the hospital's bookshelves. I want my voice to linger after I leave behind a record of my story others have typed into a database.

13. What parts of my story are written down? Who am I in the hospital's archives?

14. When a lot of grief in a soft place wants itself to be a softer place still. When all the soft places become impossible to inhabit. When the grieving body is in a hard place.

15. When the body is not hard but wants to make itself so. When I think hard is half a mile closer to invincible. When my loved ones need me to be invincible. When invincible equals miracle. When after an appointment, I am too drained to call.

16. I know they are waiting for updates of what is happening at the hospital, but I lose myself behind the blue curtain.

17. Maggie Nelson writes a book detailing all the ways she is in love with the colour blue.

18. I wonder: is there anything to love about the blue of a hospital?

19. When speech equals cannot. When a voice compels me to speak. When a pain compels me to book that appointment again.

20. Loss begins to grapple with language. Language wants to come out all at once. I am carrying my belongings from place to place. I have no extra storage for words.

21. The words gurgle an infinite arrythmia. Born in place of where my kidney once was, I might find the beginning of my story here in these lines somewhere.

22. My language doesn't want to cling to meaning anymore. It is tired like I am. It is mourning.

23. Others have written poems on love, grief and illness. This is my turn.

24. When our bodies grow weak. When disease takes hold of our organs. When our symptoms don't fit a definitive pattern for diagnosis.

25. When writing comes amid all this in recovery and passing.

26. I think, it must be by miracle that anyone can keep writing. But I follow suit in many poets' pages.

27. My words produce notes for a long lyric of grief, but my body looks for remission.

28. A surgical date before metastasis. A pill to subdue nausea. A miracle during the pandemic. A home.

THE PATIENT IS A BODY

the patient is a body is   the patient is a body is not—
a spelling test
a diagnosis
responding to treatment   please advise

the patient is a body   cannot spell
or read   or remember
at which moment the cells dividing went wrong

the patient is a body
is performance   turned list of symptoms
brain fog like someone poured cement
in skull

the patient is a body   speaks in metaphors
because fog dissipates on the tongue
but practitioners understand cement

the patient is a body
is epistemology   on medical ledgers   shorthand

the patient is a body
is digital archive   sealed from itself

the patient is a body
is process attempts to unseal itself phone call
voicemail documents pending
approval
will take eight weeks approx.

the patient is a body
enrolls in biology seminars to understand what necrosis
and papillary and lymphovascular
invasion means

the patient is a body
holds out ruler measuring 9 x 7 x 4 cm
against skin then incision on self

the patient is a body
number of years years old measuring biopolitical advantage
/ for others disadvantage

the age of the patient
is a body evading diagnosis in the first place

THIS BODY IS

this body is home to a piece of this body
is specimen 21RS-50520
labelled with the given name of this body

this body is collected sample
is addendum #1   disbelief
addendum #2   but original diagnosis remains unchanged

parts of this body are negative
parts of this body are diffusely positive

this body is whole
this body goes by one given name
except the parts of it removed

when the body sleeps   it wraps itself
in sheets of malignant cells   because without a blanket
pulled tight   everywhere else
jolts wake   freezing

Saturday mornings   this body is a red zone statistic
this body is an obstacle to healthcare
is an obstacle to this body

parts of this body   have been in a vile   a petri dish
container   specimen bag
tweezer   microscope   curve sketch
equation

simple primary school subtraction
days this body has left before metastasis
–   dates of availability in the OR

=   February might be too late

this body is still a body
in the aftermath of February

this body is a time   awaiting recovery

PRAYER ON AN OPERATING TABLE

love the red tarmac : love the heat : our bodies learning to love it : it's the only way : performances will take place : in the sun : or rain : love the stanza break : the years when nothing happened : clothing's optional : nothing's better than too many changes at once : like climate change reading : reading its love for winter : love the ground melting : under pink rosé : prescriptions for neurotransmitters diluted in alcohol : salt takes away the ground : to reveal another ground : love the taste of : what a body absorbs : at the foot of a #9 trail :

love the rain : the cognitive disassembly : in the after and now hours : the verse work : that doesn't happen but exists to love its impact : love the federal scam : love choreographer's words fabricating stories : in dream's newspaper : parts of the body that don't translate well : don't share a common language either :

love the year : of no speaking : the speaking : doesn't know what to say : except here and now : hear now : only cameras witness events : and don't register their meanings : love grapes frozen through night : fruits that do not have an end date : polaroid speaks love : for the body recovering : recovering without remembering a thing :

love the strong-bodied river : road access : not daily granted : love the body of rivers : their short-lived swimmable moments : for biodiverse species : the stones learning to blink : while the industry still remembers it as water : love the loveable moments : and grief that runs after :

love effortless childhoods : branches of moss : their own little tree : love so many beams of asphalt : the tongue becoming a highway : love medicines : options are none : Deer Lake : hope country of nowhere :

PASSAGE 4
November 2022

in one coulomb of stars
the pith of a seed calls from cyanide
and the pith of a tree
is struck   the outer edges of some
go on living   in our hearts
we call on December   moving
at a pace hard
                                        i see a Sebald
in my small kitten   born old
with white moustache and grey lanugo
reminding me of all the elders
i know   his snow falls
above the migraine of train tracks
                                                    stoic
but never cold enough
                                                    to last

my grief has become spiritual
levels   a measure leaning
religious database
of losses   always healing
inward itself
without her sense of humour—
how at the planetarium
there were the stars   and the stars
had *stopped working*—
like you i miss the already left
and leaving   all the days
it seems they are deceasing
going
                                        by us too

it all returns to Phyllis   my passages
stray from November 11
but cannot go too far   into cancer
into a day without crying
and it has only gone too far—what is
this heart for i've been numb
since twelve years old and now a planet
is tumour   is window and sounding
in me   somewhat spinning
                                                  what are
all these things
i'm feeling   language
        in the planets have not themselves
evolved   to speak

if not stars   burrow themselves
into constellations   then how
burrowing do the constant
of their experiences compare
to imaginary lines
of odes and laments we draw
stringing them across their made up
families of names
and as for others   like relatives
visit but decidedly
the sky has many countries
expanding   like us the stars
like immigrants some are too far away

we've got only the voices of poets
who've given a munificence   of their selves
away   speaking of skies in stanzas
comfort but in ways
that are never the same   *arium*
was a planet she'd invented   error
was in not leaving us a profile
of its myosin on paper   only her profile
lengths softly   scrolling
the moving eyes
of cassettes fall into place   the start
and click and reverse sounds
of dust abrading library record players
here are the voices of poets
                                        on loan for a week

talking   a loan of permanence
is not ours but the public's
to keep   we've got
only their readings now
and the evergreen mat of moss pinks
that give my anticipated nostalgia
its colour has not been decided
by spring   they read
as if every enjambment
continues as district without bend
never pausing to sound out
lines   communities
between neighbours
between metaphors and commas
never long enough
for us to disentangle their breaks

blamed time
for not giving us enough to spend
the days and years
we hoped would repeat
like Ai Qing's autumn seasons
like the life cycle
of mycelium spanning
quietly   larger than the fossils
of some dinosaurs
invisible
                                        to our memory
its body knew only
the passage of *leave this*   *leave this*
like unpacking
deciding to move again
            a set of boxes in the cells
of those   never shown time
                  some of our human kindness

i know not about sounds and laughs
heard them once or twice
from every river of person
and how those revolutionary notes
change from today and our tiny
clay-carved tomorrows
that never repeat however
we wish some days perhaps
crooning to us   perhaps returning
a head might more readily will
however we wish to see some hours
and faces again . . .
everyday architectures
a one-person cafe   visiting
relives nostalgia   with another
dearest friend

the trees   do not house us
until we turn them   into houses
nostalgia did not affect
while feeling   but
searched up its meaning
and now its meanings
house my life with such
melancholy   and loss
of loss and these days
become themselves substructure—
an architect's anticipated
nostalgic calling   meanwhile i
long grieved the passing
of this new year and i in its
sorrowful residence

i have not hoped for much
except clinging to   some remaining
beauty in loss as both
appear to me in my early twenties
mourning   the night has not
changed much from the morning
i walked out to the park
with one kidney just strong enough
to stroll   and no more
emptiness   i want   i want
to hug Rita Wong   when i remember
she who dropped a couple
berries at a reading   and left outside
to offer them as honouring
for the ancestors
                    like Phyllis
now received

PASSAGE 5
November 2024

SONNET 1

language that draws lung's bridge and beauty we fate
/ ochrea stems us   when those times we merger
too close but never decease in a dream   my kidney
is not a ghost   not necrotic sheath or ash
it has no regrets without the rest of me   no wings either
nights the body walks steady on electrolyte matter   outside
warmth already converted consonance of snow   sunlight
watered the blooms   cicadas and blue rocks planted
acrylic anaphoras repeated like poems
around the PACU   leaving us with one window's view
of the city at night surrounding a share of each other's dreams
our nurses are vowels   spaces between beds in summer ashen

SONNET 2

i would like the wind to hold me up close   please
let me inhabit your form where anything seems possible
i've tried to break things from the ground up
tried to fell a tree   if sick was a place i am still finding out
its location   this place that i'm exhausting has exhausted me
to splinters   stuck in my palm like threads in my belly
a week after surgery i renovated this flat   outside
the magnolias renovated the sky a shade of pink
temporarily   where there's wood there's a place to live
that's not a home because i'm not comfortable in this body
of medicine diluted DIY   where there's magnolias
there's something in pink that's not stitches or swelling
let me close my lungs to basement air   in wind i find
the last place that's like Georges Perec's *inventory of strictly invisible things*

SONNET 3

after Georges Perec

letters of the alphabet, words: "hang in there tiger!"
BLACKWING® 602"; "WILLIAM MORRIS Cotton Prints
"Paris 110" read upside down from the cover
of the book covering *An Attempt at Exhausting a Place in Paris*
Numbers: "73, 74, 75, 146"   *the poem:* silence is not a rest
nor eloquent   *smells:* i smell J on everything   this home
smells more like J than me because I smell like J too
grief: on book tour   on the poetry reading about grief
on the cab ride to the bookstore   coming home
while grazing a beloved's body   *in the recycling:* mail
from BC Cancer reminding me of my next CT
in my hands: dreaded locks of J's hair   i am threading new growth
through our combined past tense
sonnet: a poem about nothing   a void   a love poem

HEALING

for Dr. Truong

no,   nothing unjust about my world

that lifts me in awe of its mercy
my surgeon spends years practising

five incision points to the belly

;

this is the heart i hear
at the tempo of laparoscopic lenity   two hours

feels like seven years to my
loved ones   waiting and a lifetime
of unknowing time for the miniature robotic technology

prolonging the humanness of human life
that they can never be   and five minutes for me

i have no memory of being a part

of this world
and it feels like the closest thing i know
to dying

;

7:45 am

prepare patient to greet surgical team
and medical students   *do you watch* The Good Doctor
i ask them

this diagnosis ruined my favourite show
for me   is the body of a patient
manipulatable chemical matter   physics

though there are rules
i refuse to believe exist   the same world

that gave me a rare cancer   for my age group
gave it to me on a dispensable organ

caused an Omicron outbreak
in the hospital   but pronounced this variant if infectious
then at least less fatal

it knows there's been
so much loss already

;

we are the cells that make up the body
and memory of the world   and causes it to hurt
sometimes

;

my friend is still in the hospital room   her daughter
waiting to see her   it's been a week since her last
memory of being able to walk without pain

of cooking Chinese food   of talking to someone
no she cannot understand English   no but she has
learned to communicate with the nurses

who bring her a tray of warm soy milk

;

no nothing

unjust about this world with some hard lumps
in its body   hurting   but go on beating
its heart for us   because it doesn't want to leave

it doesn't want to let go either

;

i don't believe in luck   Dr. Truong says
but i know i am lucky

because i woke up and knew
that they are still here   and that the moment of brief
transformation from snow

to gently boughing greens of aspen
will be a long and thawing lyric by the time   we are healing

PROMISED YOU A POEM

for Linda Morra

november

november

november

everything has felt

everything entered the trees
before Montreal's branches
laid more sentences on the
yellowing ground

everyone
lined up for bagels
Sunday morning outside
along quiet corners of the rue
French radio 7 pm music
with no lyrics improved my language
of going to a city
and
wanting to fall in love
with a place slower than i
already have
wanting to
stay
wait on the lookout
where language blew
past comprehension
and i stayed behind when i left

DIAGNOSIS

Left nephrectomy:
A. High-grade renal cell carcinoma, 4.3 cm maximum gross dimension.

saline   right balance
as blood   as pH   IV external vein
searching and pricking again
after collapse like giving up   it's my body
that's tender right now,   i'm guessing
equilibrium hangs
in concentrate to show platelets
a way to regain control   of themselves
mistaken nausea
for symptoms of grief
but cancer hasn't spread
but progressed deeper into arteriole
efferent filtration

                    for a whole November
i told no one   and no one knows
now,   when   or how
it happened so quickly
                        at one point
self-love
became a requirement
of recovery   but even now
            i'm sorry   i'm struggling

;

only our emotions   have metastasized
i guess i'm lucky

most of the unwritten before
the heart waits   ten days from diagnosis
to holes in my belly and memory
hasn't processed what it's already
forgotten in a week   next to incision
the lungs email two sentences
that makes it   hard to cough or laugh
but reminds the recipient to breathe
because   i'm beginning to forget
and that's post-surgical recovery
working ,   i think
only one incision
remembers clearly   loss
of something being removed from it
and now it feels   confused
by how long its tissues are stitched / stretched

from scalpel's pressure after the others
had stopped feeling / taking notice

;

if relief came an octave sooner
there would be less deaths in the world
less news followed by the chord procession
of families crying   if illness
was a song   it would be cruel
for it to have a voice that sings   beautifully

though all of us would be singing
versions of that song

if our language had a word
for space between symptoms and diagnosis
some people would never stop singing

;

following continuity of care   is patient
sifting through archived case history
of self   while the memory blanks
body dawn   meaning
down but to begin again   encountering on films
the hilum vaguely remembering

;

found   is diagnosis falling into pattern of losses
like the stuff that centuries are made of
        here the mass
lines friable ,   necrotic at fissure   into hilum
blood chorus of vessels singing   into organ
making the kidney work   sleepless
2 am producing
urine / endless invisible blood   the patient
cannot eat or drink from nausea
IV lays off digestive tract a second day
like dress rehearsal
        for surgery perforating

abdominal mane
                    and pathology's light chain
fragments malignant sheets
bearing unusual morphological appearance

                    like all November
when words came
      in place of the poets and another
sixteenth home
      and gene expression thought about pronouncing
goodbyes   synthesized
                    longer and faster

DEAR NAN

our culture has many storytelling traditions—
Quyi, Penshui, go pick a bundle
of fresh spring onions from the street market
hand them as an offering to your nan

watch her chew the green tender leaves
before adjusting her teeth   left
in her good hand   slender white bottom frills
milder in flavour   ready to be lowered into water

my family has many storytelling traditions
but i've lost touch with all   the clouds
are almost full tonight   i find shapes in patches
of sky still left   negative spaces   gaps

in your story
where both our memories fizz   old age
upon a lost mother tongue   left for me to fill

Dear Nan,

;

dear nan   may i call you that
the names of family members are given   but
no one gave me your name   the clouds
are almost full   i look at shapes in every patch of sky
dear nan   am i telling our story right?

left side of the house where i live
is another house   i can see nothing of the sky
low living in the ground-floor basement
T.S. Eliot's *The Waste Land* sleeps under
my lampshade   i hear it snoring little poems
on the first day of April
i do not sleep   i talk to you   in me
you live here too

everything i need is here except the sky
i want to look up at something that changes
and still be comfortable   the sky has changed
Rob Nixon calls it slow violence the way
for the months of summer   there's no more rain
to feed plants who shoot little smokes
lining the sun purple   the moon red

but there are no red guards on the streets
no student picket lines around Tiananmen
your children have taken your scallions and sprouted
them far from where they think
your roots may be buried   wherever they think
those roots remain

i am making scallion pancakes
here is a plate   i am splitting them with you

;

dear nan

the words on the bus jump out at me
FOR YOUR SAFETY PLEASE HOLD ON

it's been long since i've checked my daily horoscopes
but this city   this street   the planters with baby cypress
fenced in square by orange plastic tape
are telling me to go slower

these signs birthed a generation like mine
to take up soft living
in an uninhabitable city   rent increases
no place to live   bed rotting
is a thing gen x looks forward to
nine-year-old TikTokers stream their self-care routines
some video gamers in Japan leave their homes
only at night
has soft turned us into vampires?

;

the architecture in this city
is not soft the ground where i assume you are buried
is harder still   i trip on my platform shoes
and squeeze the juices out of a bug
or maybe it was a red berry

there is violence in the slow   the soft
a personal cost wanting to appear taller   more confident
on the street
part of me still believes that if i'm tall
dressed in black   and goth
men won't approach me

out there on the street there is violence
and there are berries
in that sense nothing's changed
since your time   there is an extra inch to my height
i must walk slower
in order not to squish the remaining
of this world's soft   vulnerable things

SEVEN FLOODS

come August storm drains outside our basement
will flood we will wake up to a river kitchen
faulting our plastic slippers for not being big enough boats
two mops and a Swiffer shake their heads
as we march clumsily over two inches of rainwater
this happens every year
when summer ends and the dirt-scabbed drains from yet another
parch spell loosen this is a small price to pay

the storm carries muddied debris into our quarters
serving earth where carpet rations the wood beneath
perhaps autumn will permit dirt to take root in the crevices of plaster
the hepa seal of our hoover vacuum will rock and bloat
summoned to harvest in the aftermath of dampness
a mushroom field fungi arms webbed mycelium
reclaiming our bathroom floor tiles as their own

long days pond into each other—
lily pads expanding their thorax into the sun
blocking light for life beneath some days are like that
when floorboards heave and rest with two pair of lungs
while small details flood our homegrown sanctuary
we are a cleave poem
partners that origami during crisis diverted
enveloping each other's folds

we laugh through the dampness that lingers   for days
after the flood   after the early morning discoveries—
once a year work comes before coffee   brewed   cooling
on the table   forgotten between sips   wringing
and swapping out wet cloths

let this day go on   we dare ourselves, knowing
exhaustion like the sky that's rained itself of every drop
sweating   slipping back into bed   this is how we welcome August

FUNERAL FOR A MINK

for J

we plan funeral for a mink
Saturday behind the A&W   caught along
small stretch of dirt road forming an almost forest
my hand in yours
we, dressed in black for comfort
not planning our cherished walk side by side
sipping slushies to melt into an occasion for mourning

but mourning finds us anyway   this animal
not breathing nor in pain
already gone with the car tires
that might have collided last night or this morning
into soft animal
now tombstone   now body of loss
we had not space in our own bodies to contain—
a mink

we pluck wild grasses
and spread a quilt over its flattened belly
heads bowed ignoring dew drops that light up
spider web's christening

you lower me into the spell of your grief
                                                                        and i ask you
when was the last time you've cried

you say not since your street days
watching the body of a young man lifted
on stretcher to the hospital   learning only later
it had been your friend who passed from an overdose

grieving will be a part of our walking ritual
from now on   moving with us
concussing
howling at once past the fence two houses away
with the punctual bark of the neighbour's great dane
announcing the ordinary: a doorbell; the news

PHYLLIS WRITES, WORDS ESCAPE ME, AND I THINK, THE WORLD IS BREAKING MY HEART

first came healing   the learning that rejected ghosts as past tense
white bark coughing sap like phlegm
                    out their only unblocked airway
only it's sweeter coming out
                    of trees   this grieving that breaks
the body first
            / body senses that breathing is a precious thing
a diversion of air through the mouth
            such evolutionary mercies
    accounting for time   un-ionizing   strange evolutionary grief

;

taught me about starlings
                    the flight of one's alignment
also alignment's dialogue in flight   guided by the field of vision
                    of its seven closest kin
        that's the scientific denomination
for how communities are made
            / to us   synonym for   *it takes thousands*
to conduct magic that's the unspoken behaviour   of murmurations
            always precise   a nurtured flight

                    like one bird's call
or one poet's voice skied with rain over shelter
entering surface area of another
            / to me   magic of one influenced by thousands
by the names of Blaser   Wah   Webb   et al.

;

i call to the sun   though the star feels further away   though
it is summer aligning movement
with warmer days   small twig and yellow stone
become same shadow
inside sidewalk's heartwood—
the mature and deceased crease
of its lining
think nightjar   soil's all disappeared but shares
one body
with the pith of itself that lives

one year   grief ran its impossible course   like vocabulary
of a strong wind because the losses and their growing refrain
/ new age and newfound ache: mattered

the severity of early roseate mornings came:
mattered   while forgetting
made strange carbon atoms cry   winnowed grief
spun spore through quiet endorphins forgot

;

returned one afternoon along watershed's
grey muddied arms   scaling fence to catch night 401 bus
toward *place that's got clearest air i've ever breathed*
said Hannah

maybe it's clarity i miss   clarity people say they see in me
except now recognition of a former sweet memory

new words formed by new weather
on the forecast channel   unrecognizable past tense

how to speak the serenade of a swift-passing
beloved space

how to leave remembering
what went before genus: we call atmospheric river
or the anticipated nostalgia of leaving
like chirring calls from an ancient family of remaining arcades

MORE IMPERFECT SESTINA

for Phyllis

where are we now   hold our loved poets as seas   as oceans   close
this *imperfect sestina* choreographs   the perfect
cinematography of six-beat repetitions   musics of this life
our hearts   slow motion not repetition but a moving
forward ephemeral improv   *eyes pouring over the stone*   this heart
    do you hear the sound
of a moving toward   her *illuminations*   that *ephemeral thing*

Fred's *music at the heart of thinking*
Steve says happens *the moment a poem announces*
itself as ready to be written   *is lost now*   perhaps
lost is readiness   of the mind ghost   to unhaunt the living's
unhomed de-visioned   profiles of movement
bodies / parentheses / being to cohabit with the sound

of brackets at the music of sounding
who am i to you   to others   our common loving of mutual things
because if you are lost   how much of myself
that i recognized in you   needed of our perennial
path the signs of love and crossing   is also lost   Butler writes   when
    we lose
something we grieve   we *i* ourselves inseparable   the removal

of selves   a moving
perfect vulnerability   *bodies are submerged*   such sounds
they become the space they inhabit   [— Ahmed]   think now
while Phyllis was here   think heart   journalistic eye

slow pulsing our collective *i* we recognized in her our perfect
island congruent counterpart and friend compass point and
  means to a living

with meaning inseparable the forces of living
are meant to be broken and assembled composed moving
a reassembled broken body without her but surrounding
that *ephemeral thing* [— Barad recomposed]
Phyllis i say tell me what words you want to say up close
for the beating hearts missing you how to perfect

(if i'm worthy to know in afterlives you sea) a music imperfect
for the homeostatic quivering Elee: *of course every grief is an
  anchor line*
to previous losses island ferry rituals redefined not gone, Steve
  the poet moving
in the cities and homes and poetries of her sound
how to feed her ravens red bitter berries of winter and still feed
  everything
else up close we love Phyllis thinks we can it seems

Phyllis music toward the movement of closure
fill us music 1 2 3 . . . 7 movements toward the closed beat of
  ephemeral things

—November 22

During the summers of my undergrad at SFU, I spent my time between classes inside the Special Collections vault on the 7th floor of the library, taking advantage of the temperature-controlled room and its free air-conditioning. I found Phyllis Webb's reading of this poem on a second-generation reel-to-reel cassette, numbered #355 as part of the 5000 recordings of poetry readings, stories, lectures, conferences, birthday parties and gatherings held by BC poets from the 1960s to '90s. Visiting this room with a little portable cassette player, I was astonished by the voices of Phyllis's generation of poets and their keen practices of commemorating, collecting, taping over and trading. Phyllis's presence takes up, humbly, a mere four tapes across the entire collection. Between her readings on cassette, I emailed Steve Collis, asking, "Which book is this poem from?" Sometimes, he'd say, "I'm not sure, but it sounds familiar!" And with poet friends, I would try to track the poems down. One poem, we never were able to track down on the page.

Phyllis Webb composed "Here I am Reading at the Planetarium" for an international poetry festival taking place at the Planetarium in downtown Toronto. Phyllis, to our knowledge, read this poem twice before an audience of primarily poets but never published it; the first performance took place on the day of her Planetarium debut, and the second ensued shortly afterward on July 9, 1981 as part of her reading with the Coast is a Line series. Reanimating such rare occasion of a poetry gathering under the stars, Webb gently guided her listeners, easing them into the sound and cadence of her voice intending, as she put it, to go "easily and lightly." Among those attending were series host Roy Miki and Eli Mandel, who introduced her. Her own preface under summer daylight entangles with the hypnotic atmosphere of celestial bodies, borrowed from a seemingly refracted, immeasurable time:

> Here I am
>
> reading at the Planetarium
>
> the planet /
>
> arium
>
> arium /
>
> the planet
>
> I have just discovered
>
> in downtown Toronto
>
> STARS STARS STARS STARS
>
> Give me /
>
> poets
>
> a handful of dust
>
> before the skies
>
> fall down

Steve and I returned to this poem after Phyllis's passing on Remembrance Day, 2021. We projected a galaxy onto the office ceiling with a star light projector, which felt fitting given the "STARS STARS STARS STARS" that Phyllis projected with her voice on repeat. We decided to try our hand transcribing the poem on paper, individually at first, sifting through her books of poems, looking for clues and patterns about how she might have structured her line breaks, or ventured into experimental forms at the time she composed this poem.

When we finished transcribing, we swapped poems for the big reveal. In the epigraph of this book, Phyllis's poem is how I transcribed it. I've included Steve's here.

I still talk to Phyllis often. I tell her how her friends are doing, tell her about visiting the bowl with Fred and Pauline on Salt Spring Island and then heading over to Diana and Peter's for lunch. I tell her about the quiche that Diana made, and about how one hundred metres from where the bowl was, by the water, I tried climbing a tree to get to a tall swing and got stuck.

I got stuck a lot in the years that followed, after cancer, fatigue and the brain fog. Fred and Pauline were in a room where I had a reading.

"This is a new poem I wrote."

Fred asked, "When is your next book out?"

"Possibly never," my response, "given . . . I'm writing like about a poem a year."

When writing becomes stilted, I talk to Phyllis. She, of all people, understands the waiting when words "escape" our poet brains.

Shared grief is like a weighted blanket. It is also a collaboration in the way that the six of us shared stories by the bowl and the moment we started reading our favourite Phyllis poems, Salt Spring suddenly started hailing.

Shortly after her passing, I had a dream where Phyllis's friends were on a body of water, somewhere in Stanley Park, but under a bridge. Sitting on a log, trying not to fall off. At one point, I almost did fall. Floating in the water were a few things we had brought for her, a large shell collecting water but never sank. A cat tunnel, because Phyllis liked cats, and dreams are weird. This is shared grief. It feels heavier because we have many friends who loved Phyllis, and so the weight of all our grief is compounded. But drifting, mindlessly from shore, we won't let each other float away.

NOTES

In a book about Phyllis Webb, there are, of course, some lines borrowed from her poems.

From "Poems of Failure": *diamonds from a pattern piece / one purple one red / attach another making designs as I go*; from *Naked Poems*: *there is room;* from "Marvell's Garden": *place of solitude*; from *Sunday Water*: *take that.*

"More Imperfect Sestina" is after Phyllis's poem "Imperfect Sestina"; *solitary confinement* is after her poem "Solitary Confinement"; *talking* is from her book titled *Talking.*

past the broken shell / of her ear is a line of Phyllis's from "The Birds" in *Sunday Water* and also in Diana Hayes's book *Gold in the Shadow*.

In Constellations, Nnedi Okorafor's science fiction and the swordfish refers to her story "Moom!"

The long poems took place as a collaboration with Steve Collis, when we were both writing passages separately, but would swap poems and give each other feedback, sometimes borrowing lines. These lines are originally his: *light that remains unmade; love and love; there is love; leave this leave this; it takes thousands / to conduct magic that's the unspoken behaviour / of murmurations.*

In "Not a SpongeBob Poem," Ahmed refers to Sara Ahmed; Cecily refers to Cecily Nicholson; the lines *heal something / i had forgotten / on the far side / of the receding hill / i saw was / our only refuge* and *full bodied* is from a poem that Steve sent his friends in an email during Solstice month.

"Untitled" is a response to Otoniya J. Okot Bitek's *100 Days,* which I wrote in Sophie McCall's class and later sent to Julie.

In "More Imperfect Sestina," Ahmed again refers to Sara Ahmed; Butler refers to Judith Butler; Barad refers to Karen Barad; Elee refers to Elee Kraljii Gardiner; Fred Wah and his book *Music at the Heart of Thinking* also make an appearance; I think *path the signs of love and crossing* is either Fred's or Steve's line; *eyes pouring over the stone* is possibly Phyllis's. Oh dear.

ACKNOWLEDGEMENTS

Thank you everyone who appears in this book. Thank you Janine Young, Silas White and the entire Nightwood team for your support and belief in me.

Thank you Dr. Thyer and Dr. Truong for saving my life. Thank you to my friends and community for your prayers, kind messages and wishes, and support after my cancer diagnosis, and those of you who helped with meals, rides and a safe place to stay during that time. And thank you to all those who visited me when I was stuck at home and depressed.

I am grateful to the Writers' Trust Woodcock Grant. As well, my gratitude to the editorial teams at *Event Magazine*, SFU Gallery, *Ampersand Review* and *ARC* for publishing earlier versions of some poems. Also, my love and appreciation to the reading series who invited me, where I was able to share this new body of work, and those in the audiences who listened.

Thanks to Mercedes Eng, SFU English writer-in-residence, who gave me feedback on "this body is," "the patient is a body," and "Phyllis Writes, Words Escape Me, and I Think, the World Is Breaking My Heart." And Maria Barraza, for introducing me to Nnedi Okorafor's writing. "Moom!" is my favourite short story.

Many thanks to my oddly concocted family for saving me many and many times over. Catherine and Richard, my foster parents, who loved me even after I mixed bleach and Clorox and made toxic chlorine gas in their apartment on Christmas Eve. Isabelle Hebert, who teaches me adult life skills like how you should not mix cleaning chemicals because that will make chlorine gas. Necole, my mother-in-law with three sons, but I'm her favourite child. Josh Hoskins, my fiancé, who after hearing me read "Seven Floods" at a reading said, "You never work before coffee." He of all people would know, because he brings me my coffees in the morning. But shhh! You are spilling my secrets! Thank you Dany Loki Chaos, my cat who is blocking the computer screen as I am editing this. Nimbus Sebald Puff, cat #2 who is perfect and never blocks my screens. Kendall, cat of sixteen years old who loves Josh and tolerates me.

And more thanks to those who have offered wisdom, friendship, conversations and love. I can't name everybody, but here goes trying. My bestie, Mia Kartodirdjo. LJ Weisberg. Cassandra Blanchard. Jaimie and Jonathan. Jonina Kirton. Diana Solomon. Erik Christenson. Lindsey Freeman. Melek Ortabasi. Mark Deggan. Steve Collis. Sophie McCall. Jesse Wong. Ronna Bloom. Linda Morra. Rina Chua. Appa and family. *poetry in canada* crew. Natalie Lim. Jinnie Saran. Phoebe Wang. Josephine Wang. Joanne Leow. Alexandra Lesk. The entire SA 856 class of Spring 2025.

ABOUT THE AUTHOR

Photo credit: LJ Weisberg

Isabella Wang is the author of *Pebble Swing* (Nightwood, 2021), a finalist for the Dorothy Livesay Poetry Prize, and the chapbook *On Forgetting a Language* (Baseline Press, 2019). Among other recognitions, she has been shortlisted for *Arc*'s Poem of the Year Contest, *The Malahat Review*'s Far Horizons Award for Poetry and Long Poem Contest, *Minola Review*'s Inaugural Poetry Contest, and was the youngest writer to be shortlisted twice for *The New Quarterly*'s Edna Staebler Personal Essay Contest. In 2025, she was named one of the Writers' Trust Rising Stars. Wang's poetry and prose have appeared in over thirty literary journals and five anthologies, including *Watch Your Head: Writers and Artists Respond to the Climate Crisis* (Coach House Books, 2020), *They Rise Like a Wave: An Anthology of Asian American Women Poets* (Blue Oak Press, 2021) and *The Spirits Have Nothing to Do with Us: New Chinese-Canadian Writers Fiction* (Wolsak & Wynn, 2022). She is the web coordinator for *poetry in canada*, and directs her own non-profit editing and mentorship program, Revise-Revision Street.